Mass Extinctions

Christopher Lampton

MASS EXTINCTIONS

One Theory of Why the Dinosaurs Vanished

Franklin Watts
New York/London/Toronto/Sydney
An Impact Book

1986

Diagram on page 14 is from Don L. Eicher,
Geologic Time © 1976, p. 152. Adapted by permission
of Prentice-Hall, Englewood Cliffs, New Jersey.

Diagrams on pp. 17 and 78 first appeared in
New Scientist, London, The Weekly Review of
Science and Technology, 8 November 1984.

Diagram on p. 51 is redrawn from "The End of the
Cretaceous Sharp Boundary or Gradual Transition?",
Alvarez. W., et al, *Science*, Vol. 223, Fig. 1, p. 1184,
16 March 1984. Copyright 1984 by the AAAS.

Diagram on pp. 66-67 is from "How a Star Can Cause
Devastation," by David Sutter, December 18, 1984.
Copyright © 1984 by The New York Times Company.
Reprinted by permission.

Diagram on p. 72 is from Kauffman, original, in press.

Illustration on page 81 is from "The Mass Extinctions
of the Late Mesozoic," by Dale A. Russell. Copyright
1982 by Scientific American, Inc. All rights reserved.

Photographs courtesy of Richard Faverty
© *Discover* Magazine, May 1984, Time Inc.: p. 18;
American Museum of Natural History: pp. 24 (#32854),
46 (#322113); The Yerkes Observatory: p. 35;
Doddy and Zeller © *Discover* Magazine,
May 1984, Time Inc.: p. 36; William Clemens ©
Discover Magazine, May 1984, Time Inc.: p. 52 (top);
Erle Kauffman: p. 52 (bottom).

Library of Congress Cataloging in Publication Data
Lampton, Christopher.
Mass extinctions.

(An Impact book)
Bibliography: p.
Includes index.
Summary: Explains various theories about how
dramatic changes in the earth's surface could have
caused periodic mass extinctions, with an emphasis
on the disappearance of the dinosaurs.
1. Extinction (Biology)—Juvenile literature.
2. Comets—Juvenile literature. 3. Iridium—Juvenile
literature. [1. Extinction (Biology) 2. Dinosaurs.
3. Catastrophes (Geology)] I. Title.
QE721.2.E97L35   1986   560   86-5634
ISBN 0-531-10238-6

Contents

Mass Extinctions

Chapter

1

Death in the Ancient Past

Buried within the earth is a book that will reveal the secrets of the ages to anyone who knows how to read it.

It is not written on paper, nor is it written in any language spoken on earth today. It is called the *fossil record*, and it is made up of the bones, footprints, and petrified remains of plants and animals that lived in the prehistoric past. The story told by the fossil record stretches over more than half a billion years. It is one of the most important stories ever told and one of the most fascinating. It is the story of life on earth. In some ways, it is a mystery story.

For more than a century, scientists who call themselves *paleontologists* have been translating this record so that it can be read by those of us not familiar with the language of fossils. The translation is a slow, painstaking task, in part because the fossil record is not complete. Only a tiny fraction of living organisms in the prehistoric past left behind remains for paleontologists to dig up, and those remains are buried within the very rocks of the earth itself.

From this fossil record, we can learn several important things. The first lesson we learn is that living organisms change with time. The kinds of plants and animals that lived on earth millions of years ago are not the same as the kinds that live on earth today. And yet every organism alive today is a descendant of some organism that lived on earth then. The slow process of change that altered those ancient life forms, generation by generation, into the ones we see today is called *evolution*. In general, evolution is the process by which new species—that is, distinct types of organisms—arise out of old species and by which the new species adapt to the way in which they can make a "living" in the world. The way a species makes its living—the type of food it eats, the way it gathers that food, the way it gives birth to and nurtures its young, the way it avoids being eaten by predators, and so forth—is called its *ecological niche*. Evolution permits a species to adapt, over time, to a particular ecological niche.

The second important thing we learn from the fossil record is that living species have a definite life span, just as individual members of the species do. They are born—through evolution—they live on earth for a span of time, and they die. The death of a species is called an *extinction*. Most of the species that have evolved and lived on earth in its long history are now extinct—that is, dead.

Why do species become extinct? The fossil record does not say, but paleontologists have ventured a number of theories. One theory is that an older species may find itself in competition with a newer species, a species that has recently evolved, for a particular ecological niche. For instance, both species may eat the same food, and that food may be in limited supply. If the newer species is better at gathering food than the older species, the newer species will thrive and the older species may eventually die out because it cannot compete successfully in that environment.

The most dramatic extinctions, however, are the so-called *mass extinctions*, when hundreds of species disappear from the fossil record in the course of only a few million years, the mere blink of an eye to a paleontologist. What causes these mass extinctions? No one knows—and that is why the story told by the fossil record is a mystery story, one for which no detective has yet offered a satisfactory solution. One possibility is that the environment in which these species lived was suddenly and dramatically altered, causing thousands of species to lose the ecological niches to which evolution had so painstakingly adapted them. Those species that could not adapt to new environments became extinct—and the course of life on earth was forever changed. And what brought about these changes? The nineteenth-century anatomist Georges Cuvier believed that they were the result of abrupt "revolutions," or catastrophes, that killed off large numbers of living creatures making way for the evolution of new and different organisms. Cuvier's theory came to be known as *catastrophism*.

In time, however, geologists showed that slow processes of change were at work within the earth that could alter the environment over long periods of time without the intervention of any single great catastrophe. These slow processes of change seemed adequate to explain the mass extinctions in the fossil record, and so paleontologists adopted the concept of *gradualism*, which held that changes in the nature of life on earth come slowly, over many thousands of years. There were no sudden catastrophes. Although mass extinctions might seem like sudden events on superficial examination of the fossil record, they were actually gradual processes that might have taken several million years.

The earth is more than 4½ billion years old. To the best of our knowledge, life on earth began about 4 billion years ago. The first known living "creatures" were little more than molecules—chains of atoms—floating in the ocean. What distinguished these living molecules from nonliving molecules was their ability to make copies of themselves—that is, to reproduce. Inevitably, the oceans started to fill with copies of these molecules, competing with one another for food, the raw materials necessary for making new copies of themselves. Of course, not all copies were perfect, and a few of the imperfect copies were actually improvements on the original. Because the improved copies were better at gathering food and making copies of themselves, they soon came to outnumber their unimproved cousins. Thus began the process of evolution, which is still going on today.

In time, these primeval organisms became more complex, until they resembled the one-celled organisms that you can see in a drop of pond water placed under a microscope. Some of the one-celled organisms must have then grouped together to form multicelled organisms, perhaps similar to the modern jellyfish. For the first 3½ billion years that organisms existed on earth, however, they must have remained in essentially soft-bodied forms, for they left behind few fossils. For this reason, paleontologists sometimes refer to this 3½-billion-year period as the *cryptozoic age*—the age of "hidden life."

One-half billion years ago, however, life exploded across the face of the earth and began leaving fossils aplenty. The time period from the beginning of this explosion to the present is called the *phanerozoic age*— the age of "evident life."

The phanerozoic age is divided by paleontologists into three eras—the *Paleozoic* ("ancient life"), the *Mesozoic* ("middle life"), and the *Cenozoic* ("recent life"). These eras are in turn divided into periods. See the chart on page 14 for a complete list of these eras and periods, which altogether make up the *geologic time scale*. This is the "calendar" that paleontologists use to measure time in the ancient past.

These periods and eras are not arbitrary demarcations of time. The borders between periods and eras represent significant events in the history of life—and some of these events are mass extinctions. The greatest mass extinction of all occurred at the end of the Paleozoic era. Near the end of this era, more than 90 percent of the species living on earth vanished from the fossil record, within roughly 4 million years. This is sometimes called the Great Permian Extinction, the Permian being the last period of the Paleozoic era.

Another major extinction occurred at the end of the next era, the Mesozoic era. This Great Cretaceous Extinction—the Cretaceous, as you might guess, was the last period of the Mesozoic—is probably the most famous of all mass extinctions because it wiped out the great reptiles known popularly as the dinosaurs.

Other less dramatic mass extinctions occurred at the ends of several periods within the Paleozoic and the Mesozoic eras, including the Cambrian, the Ordovician, the Devonian, and the Triassic.

What caused these extinctions? There are many theories. Perhaps it was some dramatic alteration in the earth's surface—newly-formed mountains, changes in the level of the ocean, and related changes in weather—

GEOLOGIC TIME SCALE

Era	Period	Epoch	Duration in Millions of Years (Approx.)	Millions of Years Ago (Approx.)
Cenozoic	Quaternary	Recent	Approx. last 5,000 years	
		Pleistocene	2.5	—2.5—
	Tertiary	Pliocene	4.5	—7—
		Miocene	19	—26—
		Oligocene	12	—38—
		Eocene	16	—54—
		Paleocene	11	—65—
Mesozoic	Cretaceous		71	—136—
	Jurassic		54	—190—
	Triassic		35	—225—
Paleozoic	Permian		55	—280—
	Carboniferous — Pennsylvanian		45	—325—
	Carboniferous — Mississippian		20	—345—
	Devonian		50	—395—
	Silurian		35	—430—
	Ordovician		70	—500—
	Cambrian		70	—570—
	Precambrian		4,030	

Formation of Earth's crust about 4,600 million years ago

or possibly a shifting in the arrangement of the continents. The extinction of the dinosaurs could have been brought about by increased competition with other species, such as our own ancestors, the early mammals.

Until recently, though, it was an article of faith among paleontologists that each mass extinction was a separate event with its own unique cause. Even if a satisfactory explanation were to be provided for one mass extinction, it would not necessarily serve to explain any of the others, except perhaps in principle. After all, these episodes of mass extinction were separated in time by millions of years, and there could be no direct connection between them.

Or could there be?

Recently, evidence has surfaced that perhaps as many as ten mass extinctions indicated by the fossil record may have a common cause and that these extinctions may occur on a regular time schedule. Further, the ultimate cause of these extinctions might lie far beyond the planet Earth, perhaps even in interstellar space.

This theory of *periodic mass extinctions* has not yet been proved, and it may never be. It could turn out to be a simple misinterpretation of paleontological evidence. Still, even the possibility that such a thing may be true has sent ripples of excitement and controversy through two scientific fields: paleontology and astronomy. It could dramatically alter our knowledge of the way in which life evolved on this planet, as well as our view of the universe around us. Further, it could mean that Cuvier was right after all: the earth's past may be a history of one catastrophe after another.

John Sepkoski, Jr., is a paleontologist at the University of Chicago with a particular interest in the life spans of fossil species. In the early 1980s, he compiled a study of the life spans of thirty-five hundred families of sea-dwelling animals over a 250-million-year period, cataloging the point in time at which each family of organisms appeared in the fossil record and the point at which it disappeared, i.e., became extinct. With the aid of fellow paleontologist David Raup, Sepkoski then set out to analyze this data mathematically.

Raup's particular interest was in extinctions. To get a better feel for the way in which organisms became extinct, he drew a graph based on all of the extinctions in the Sepkoski study from the end of the Permian period to the present. (See page 17.) To no one's surprise, the graph showed that the rate of extinction increased sharply at certain points; these were the mass extinctions with which all paleontologists are familiar. What *was* surprising about the graph was that it showed more periods of mass extinction than paleontologists had previously been aware of, and they seemed to occur at regular intervals. When Raup and Sepkoski put the data through computer analysis, it indicated that extinction rates seemed to increase dramatically at intervals of roughly 26 million years, with the most recent such extinction occurring roughly 13 million years ago.

Raup and Sepkoski were startled. A few years earlier two paleontologists at Princeton University had suggested that mass extinctions occurred at 32-million-year intervals, but the evidence for this idea was weak, and it was dismissed by most other paleontologists because there seemed to be no good explanation of why mass extinctions should occur in such a manner. But now Raup and Sepkoski had uncovered clear evidence that mass extinctions were indeed periodic and that they occurred in a regular cycle. Such evidence cried out for an explanation.

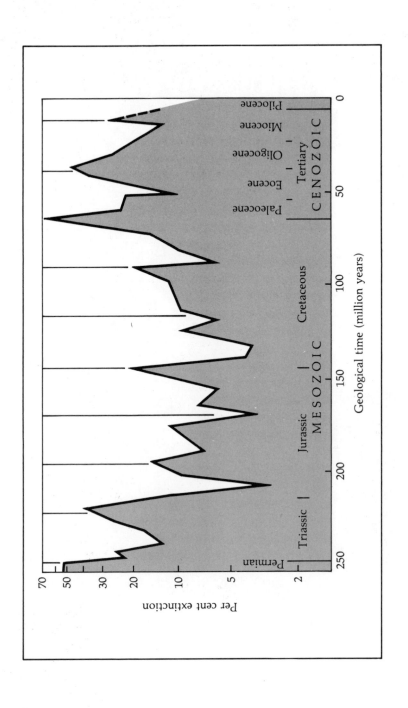

But what kind of explanation could there be? What mysterious force could wipe out large numbers of living species on such a time schedule?

When scientists discover an unexplained cycle of events—that is, an event or events that take place on a regular schedule—they like to correlate the unexplained cycle with other, well-understood cycles. There are many well-understood cycles in earthly life. Our planet rotates on its axis once every twenty-four hours, and thus we have the familiar cycle of day and night. The earth also revolves around the sun once every 365 days, and thus we have the cycle of the year and its seasons.

There are longer cycles as well, though they are somewhat less familiar. For instance, the earth's axis of rotation—the imaginary line around which it spins—is constantly (if gradually) changing its orientation in space. This is called the *precession of the equinoxes*, and it takes about twenty-six thousand years to complete the cycle.

There are no earthly cycles that require as long as a million years, however, and certainly none that would require 26 million years. No known cycles, anyway.

To find cycles long enough to associate with the periodic extinctions noted by Raup and Sepkoski, it is necessary to look beyond this planet and into the depths of space. Raup and Sepkoski were aware of this. In early 1984, when they published the results of their studies in

David Raup, left, and John Sepkoski, who discovered the 26-million-year cycle of mass extinctions

The Proceedings of the National Academy of Sciences, they wrote:

> If the forcing agent [behind the extinctions] is in the physical environment, does this reflect an earthbound process or something in space? If the latter, are the extraterrestrial influences solar, solar system, or galactic? Although none of these alternatives can be ruled out now, we favor extraterrestrial causes for the reason that purely biological or earthbound physical cycles seem incredible, where the cycles are of fixed length and measured on a time scale of tens of millions of years. By contrast, astronomical and astrophysical cycles of this order are plausible even though candidates for the particular cycle observed in the extinction data are few.

In other words, if there were to be an explanation for the cycle that Raup and Sepkoski had observed in mass extinctions, it was not likely to come from scientists who studied the planet Earth. Rather, it would come from scientists who studied the stars, and thus the ball was passed to astronomers.

This was an incredible, almost science-fiction notion, that the history of life might be tied to some force from outer space. To make sense of this idea, we must step back for a moment from our discussion of extinctions on earth and take a look at the wider universe of which our planet is only a very small part.

Chapter

2

The Beginning
of Time

Fifteen billion years ago (give or take 5 billion years), all of the matter in our universe was crammed into a single point in space, infinitesimally small—or so most scientists believe, based on persuasive evidence. How it got there we do not know, nor do we know how long it remained that way. Apparently at some point there was a tremendous explosion that pushed this matter outward in all directions from that original point. In that explosion, which we call the *big bang*, the universe as we know it was created.

If you stand outside on a dark, clear night and look up at the sky, you can see a tiny patch of the universe that was formed in that big bang. The first thing you probably will notice about the universe is that it is full of bright, luminous stars. The second thing you'll notice is that it is also full of black, empty space.

There is a lot more to the universe, though, than we can see with our naked eyes. Astronomers use instruments called *telescopes* to study the universe in greater detail.

Telescopes come in several varieties. Most of us are familiar with optical telescopes, which use lenses and mirrors to capture light from the stars and from other bright objects in space. Optical telescopes show us what these objects would look like if we could see them from a closer vantage point. With the aid of an instrument called a *spectroscope*, they can also tell us what these objects are made of and how fast they are moving. Radio telescopes, on the other hand, capture radio waves produced by objects in space. Radio telescopes can't show us what the objects look like, but they can give us lots of other useful information about them. There are also telescopes that capture gamma rays, X-rays, and infrared light from outer space, and each of these instruments tells astronomers something different and important about the objects they are observing.

The astronomer generally uses the telescope in conjunction with a camera so that there is a permanent photographic record of the information received from space. In photographs of the sky, we can see that our universe contains more than just stars and empty space.

Among other things, it contains *galaxies*. Galaxies are great islands of stars, floating in space. Most of the stars in the universe are grouped together in galaxies. The typical galaxy is immense, larger than our imaginations can conceive, so large that a ray of light takes hundreds of millions of years to cross from one end to the other. (By contrast, a ray of light takes about 9 minutes to travel from the sun to the earth and about 1½ seconds to travel from the earth to the moon.) For that reason, we say that the typical galaxy is several hundred million *light-years* across. Galaxies come in several different shapes. Most galaxies are giant spirals, but a few are elliptical in shape and others are irregular clouds of stars.

Our own sun is a star, and it is part of a galaxy. You can see that galaxy with your naked eyes on a clear night, as a wide luminous strip stretching across the sky from one horizon to the other. We call this luminous strip the Milky Way, and thus we call our galaxy the Milky Way galaxy. As seen from earth, it looks quite different from other galaxies because we are seeing it from *inside*. However, the illustration on page 24 shows you what it might look like if we could see it from a more distant perspective.

Like many of the galaxies we can see through telescopes, the Milky Way galaxy is spiral in shape. The "arms" of the spiral are made up of stars, and the dark areas between the arms are filled with gas and dust. Because this combination of gas and dust is cold, it does not produce light and therefore is effectively invisible. Many of the dark areas of space that we glimpse through our telescopes (and even with the naked eye) are filled with such dark matter. In fact, astronomers have only recently begun to recognize that "invisible" matter of one kind or another makes up more than 90 percent of the universe we live in.

Not all of the dark matter in our galaxy is located in between the spiral arms. Much of it is in the *galactic plane*. The galactic plane is not a thing but a place. Put the palms of your hands together in front of you. If your two hands together represent the disk of our galaxy, with the center of the spiral located at approximately your middle knuckles, then the narrow space between your palms is the galactic plane. It is here that much of the loose debris in the galaxy settles out, including a lot of gas and dust. Believe it or not, some astronomers have implicated this loose debris as a possible cause of Raup and Sepkoski's periodic extinctions. More about this will be discussed in Chapter Four.

The Milky Way Galaxy

Our own sun is located out toward the fringes of the Milky Way galaxy, in one of the spiral arms. It is not a first-generation star—that is, it was not born at the same time as the galaxy itself, shortly after the big bang. Rather, it was born almost 5 billion years ago out of a cloud of dust and gas much like the ones that float between the spiral arms and in the galactic plane. This cloud of gas and dust was large, several light-years across. It hung in space roughly where our sun is today, though it was much, *much* larger than the sun. Most of the gas in this cloud was a type of gas that we call *hydrogen*.

How can a star form out of a cloud of gas and dust? The answer is twofold: *gravity* and *fusion*.

Gravity is the force that holds the universe together. All matter produces gravity, and the more matter an object has in it, the more gravity it produces. A small object, like a book or a human being, produces very little gravity. A large object, like a planet or a star, produces quite a lot.

Gravity is an *attractive* force. An object that produces gravity—which is to say, any object—attracts other objects to itself. A large object like a planet or a star has a very powerful gravitational attraction. That is why we cannot fly into space whenever we feel like it by simply jumping into the air; the earth's powerful gravity pulls us right back to the ground. Rockets that escape from the earth's gravity do so only by expending huge amounts of energy to resist the attractive force. When an object such as a meteor passes near our planet, it is pulled by gravity from its normal path and into a collision course with the earth.

Like almost everything else in the universe, clouds of dust and gas in space are made up of tiny particles called *atoms*. The cloud from which our sun formed was made mostly of *hydrogen atoms*. Like any other object, an atom produces gravity, though not very much. However, the cloud from which our sun was formed contained a lot of atoms, and together they produced quite a lot of gravity. An object passing near this cloud would have found itself attracted by the cloud, just as it might be attracted by a planet or star.

The atoms in this cloud also attracted one another. Under normal circumstances this attraction wouldn't have been important because each atom in the cloud would have been simultaneously attracted by atoms to all sides of it, and thus the attractions would have canceled each other out. If something had disturbed the cloud, however, some atoms would have been able to exert more attraction than others, and the cloud would have begun to collapse. The atoms in the cloud would have drawn closer together under their mutual gravitational attraction, and the cloud would have grown smaller and smaller, with the atoms becoming more and more tightly packed together.

Apparently something—perhaps the explosion of a nearby star or a collision with another cloud of atoms—did disturb that particular cloud because it did indeed collapse. It was not a rapid collapse, like the roof of a house collapsing under a heavy snowfall. Rather, it was an extremely slow collapse that must have taken millions and millions of years.

As the cloud collapsed and the atoms in the cloud drew closer together, collisions between atoms became common. These collisions produced heat, just as you can produce heat by rubbing sticks or stones together. In time, these collisions produced so much heat that the cloud began to glow.

At this point, the cloud was very much like a star: it was hot and it produced light. In fact, it was what astronomers call a *protostar*—a star about to be born.

When hydrogen atoms within the protostar collided with one another, they were not damaged in any way, as two automobiles would be if they collided. Rather, the atoms simply bounced apart, essentially unharmed. However, as the protostar grew hotter and hotter, the collisions between atoms grew more and more violent. Eventually, a temperature was reached at which the collisions between hydrogen atoms became so violent that the colliding atoms were actually broken apart by the collisions. Such broken atoms are highly unstable, however, and so the pieces of the colliding atoms immediately reassembled to form new atoms. But in the course of a collision between hydrogen atoms, a brand-new *type* of atom was formed that was larger than the original atoms. They were *helium atoms.*

The process by which hydrogen atoms fuse together into helium atoms is called *hydrogen fusion.* More is produced by this fusion than just brand-new helium atoms. A tiny portion of the original hydrogen atoms is converted into pure energy, energy that shoots away from the helium atoms at the speed of light.

When the hydrogen fusion process began in the protostar, it was as though a switch had been thrown somewhere in the cosmos. The protostar now had a powerful, durable source of energy, a source that would keep it hot and glowing for billions of years. The protostar had become a real star—our sun.

Our sun is not alone in its small portion of the galaxy. It is only a part, albeit far and away the largest part, of a larger complex that we call the *solar system.* This complex consists of the sun, nine planets (including the one on which we live), and a diverse assortment of cosmic debris. The nine planets, as well as a goodly portion of the debris, spin around the sun in circular paths called *orbits.* In order, moving outward from the sun, the nine planets are Mercury, Venus, Earth, Mars, Jupiter, Saturn, Uranus, Neptune, and Pluto. (Actually, Pluto's highly irregular orbit has temporarily moved it inside the orbit of Neptune, so that it is currently the eighth planet and Neptune is the ninth. But the order as listed above is the one traditionally offered for the planets of the solar system.)

Where did these planets come from? Apparently, while the protostar was busily forming into a star, another process was going on nearby: the formation of planets. We don't know as much about this process as we do about the formation of the protostar because we have never observed it in action. (We *have* observed the process of protostar formation elsewhere in the galaxy, through telescopes.) However, we can theorize as to how the planets formed.

Apparently the original cloud that gave birth to our sun was rotating slowly in space when the collapse began. As the cloud collapsed and grew smaller, it began to spin faster, just as a figure skater spins faster with arms held close to the body than with arms extended. By the time it had collapsed to the size of the protostar, it was spinning very rapidly. Centrifugal force pulled much of the material of the cloud into a spinning disk surrounding the protostar. At that point the cloud must have resembled a miniature galaxy, with the protostar as the center of the galaxy and the disk surrounding it as the spiral arms.

The disk never grew hot enough for hydrogen fusion to begin. In fact, it probably began to cool off, because the atoms in the disk were stretched out very thinly compared with the atoms in the protostar. As it cooled, grains of dust began to stick together, to form lumps of rock in the disk. These rocks eventually became planets.

These early planets were surrounded by shells of gas, drawn from the original cloud and attracted to the rocky lumps by their gravity. However, the innermost planets—the ones closest to the sun—would have had difficulty holding onto their shells.

Just before hydrogen fusion began in the protostar, it would have grown very hot from the friction heat created during its collapse. This heat would have propelled streams of tiny *subatomic particles*—particles smaller than atoms—outward from the protostar. Scientists refer to this stream of particles as the *T Tauri wind*. Although it would have stopped blowing as soon as the fusion reactions began in the protostar, the T Tauri wind was sufficient to destroy the gas shells surrounding the inner planets. (Most of the planets later gained thinner shells of gas as volcanoes released gases that had been imprisoned within them during their formation. This is the original source of the air that we breathe, although it was originally made up of a very different assortment of gases.) Because the T Tauri wind could not reach past the four innermost planets, the planets beyond that point would have retained thick shells of gas.

That pretty much explains the way our solar system looks today. The sun is at the center—the sun we see in the sky every day, formed from the original protostar. The nine planets revolve around the sun, formed from the disk of gas and dust surrounding the protostar. The four innermost planets—Mercury, Venus, Earth, and Mars—are small and rocky, with thin *atmospheres* (shells of gas), formed by volcanic action. These are the planets (known as the terrestrial planets) that were stripped of their original gaseous shells by the T Tauri wind. The next four planets—Jupiter, Saturn, Uranus, and Neptune—are huge, but they consist mostly of gas and ice, with rocky cores that may be no larger than the four innermost planets. They are the planets that retained their original atmospheres. Only Pluto fails to fit this picture. It is small and rocky like the planets of the inner solar system. Some astronomers have gone so far as to suggest that Pluto was not part of the original solar system formed from the protostar's disk but was somehow added to the solar system at a later date.

And what about the debris we mentioned? There's a lot of it. For instance, between the orbits of Mars and Jupiter is a ring of rocks called the *asteroid belt*. The asteroids may be the remnants of a planet that never quite formed while the other planets were developing from the spinning cloud.

There may be another ring, or sphere, of debris far beyond the orbit of Pluto. When the original cloud of gas and dust collapsed to form our solar system, some of the gas and dust around the edges of the cloud may not have been caught in the collapse. Instead, that gas and dust may still be floating in space, in more or less its original form, way out at the fringes of our solar system, one or two light-years from the sun. In fact, this debris may form a giant shell around our solar system, a sphere that encloses our sun and all the planets.

We cannot see this sphere with our telescopes. We can only guess that it is there on the basis of evidence that will be presented in the next chapter. It may be difficult to see how such a distant sphere of debris could be relevant to the subject of life on the planet Earth, but in fact there are astronomers who have seriously proposed that this debris from the outer solar system, left over from the birth of the solar system itself, is occasionally flung inward toward the planet Earth, where it rains fiery death on millions of living creatures.

Chapter

3

Messengers
of Disaster

The idea that something in outer space could cause death and destruction here on earth is not new. In fact, it is very old. Historically, the astronomical object that has been accused most often of bringing disasters to our planet is the *comet*. Although most of these accusations are based on superstition, a few may be grounded in fact.

Comets are part of the solar system "debris" that were discussed in the last chapter. They are chunks of frozen gas and dust—"dirty snowballs," as astronomer Fred Whipple once called them—that move around the sun in very stretched out orbits. So unusual are these orbits that a typical comet will pass very close to the sun at one end of its orbit and disappear into the outer reaches of the solar system at the other. A comet may take anywhere from decades to hundreds of thousands of years to complete one full trip through the solar system. As they near the sun, the more spectacular comets will sprout long, luminous "tails"—actually streams of particles blown off the comet by radiation from the sun.

The most famous of all comets, and one of the most spectacular, is Halley's Comet, which comes near to the sun once every seventy-six years. You may have seen it yourself, since Halley's was making one of its infrequent visits to our portion of the solar system even as this book was rolling off the printing presses, although it was not as vivid in appearance this time as during some earlier apparitions, such as that of 1910. It is named for the great eighteenth-century astronomer Edmund Halley (rhymes with "valley"), who was the first person to understand the way comets orbit the sun and the first person to recognize that many of the comets observed in the historical past, previously believed to be different comets, were actually the same comet returning again and again to the inner solar system.

Centuries before Halley, it was believed that comets were strange and disturbing messengers of doom, perhaps sent by the gods to warn the human race of impending disaster or momentous events. It is not hard to understand why people would have felt that way. Astronomers, even in the ancient past, understood that most objects in the sky move along regular, predictable paths. The stars rise and set punctually every night, as does the sun every day. The earth's moon follows its own monthly course through the sky, and each of the planets that can be seen with the naked eye has a regular schedule as well. The courses of all of these objects had been plotted by observers long before written history began.

Comets are different. They come and go at unpredictable times—or so it seemed to the ancient astronomers. (Halley eventually showed that some comets could indeed be predicted—in fact, he predicted the return of the comet that bears his name, though he did not live to see it—but the ancient astronomers can be forgiven for not noticing this.) It had to be assumed, then, that comets were not like other objects in the sky. In fact, it was believed by some observers, including the Greek philosopher Aristotle, that they were some kind of fire in the earth's atmosphere, completely apart from other things in the heavens.

Because comets were unpredictable and frightening, they were blamed for any number of terrible things that happened on earth. In its time, Halley's comet was accused of precipitating the fall of Constantinople in 1456 and the sacking of the Roman Empire by Attila the Hun in the year 451. Another comet, in 44 B.C., was implicated in the assassination of Julius Caesar.

Of course, comets were occasionally associated with joyous events as well. It has been suggested, for instance, that Halley's comet may have been the famous Star of Bethlehem, which supposedly heralded the birth of Jesus Christ. In fact, the Italian artist Giotto depicted the Star of Bethlehem as a comet, probably Halley's, in his religious painting *The Adoration of the Magi*. (Giotto probably saw Halley's comet when it passed near the earth in 1301.)

William the Conqueror declared that the appearance of Halley's comet in 1066 foretold his impending victory in the invasion of England—and, indeed, he handily defeated Harold of England later that year in the Battle of Hastings. (Whether this was a joyous event or a disaster depends on which side you were rooting for in the battle.) That appearance of Halley's comet is vividly depicted in the Bayeux Tapestry, which contains scenes of this invasion of England.

Was there any *real* connection between comets and these historical events? No, except that the belief in the power of comets might have inspired individuals into action. Perhaps the appearance of Halley's comet helped William the Conqueror mobilize a larger army in his battle against Harold; in that sense, the comet may have made a difference in history. But there was no direct cause and effect between the appearance of Halley's and other comets and the wars and deaths with which they have been associated. By Halley's time, most educated people understood that comets did not influence the course of human events in any mystical way.

But there was still the lingering possibility that comets could have a direct physical effect on the earth and its atmosphere and thereby indirectly affect life on this planet. When Halley's comet passed near the sun in 1910, for instance, astronomers predicted that the earth would pass through its glowing tail. Some people feared that poisonous gases in the comet's tail would pollute the earth's atmosphere. This did not happen because the gases in the comet's tail were much too thin to have a noticeable effect on the air that we breathe. Nonetheless, the fear of "comet poisoning" caused a certain amount of panic.

Although supposedly based on "scientific predictions," this fear of comet poisoning was really the same kind of superstitious fear that had struck observers of earlier comets in supposedly less rational times. Still, there may be a real connection between comets and disastrous events on earth.

Two years before Halley's comet appeared in 1910, the earth may have collided with a comet, or with a piece of one. On June 30, 1908, there was a tremendous explosion deep within an unpopulated region of Siberia called Tunguska. No one was killed in the explosion, but trees were flattened for 20 miles (32 km) on all sides,

Halley's Comet, photographed in May, 1911

Barringer Crater in Arizona. This crater was formed 25,000 years ago by a 150-foot (45 meters) iron asteroid that punched a hole in the earth measuring 600 feet deep (180 meters) and three-quarters of a mile wide (over 1 kilometer).

and a large herd of reindeer was destroyed. What caused the explosion? Nobody knows for sure, but the most likely theory is that a small object from space—perhaps a meteorite, asteroid or comet—crashed into the earth's atmosphere and exploded in a fiery burst of friction heat. A comet called Encke's Comet was known to be passing near the earth at the time, and a fragment of that comet could have broken off and intercepted the orbit of our planet.

We are fortunate that this fragment did not crash into a populated portion of the earth's surface, more fortunate still that it was only a fragment of the comet and not its entire bulk. However, if fragments of comets have collided with the earth within this very century, it is reasonable to assume that other fragments of comets, and even entire comets, have collided with the earth in the distant past.

And, in fact, there is evidence that this is so. Many craters have been found on earth that appear to have been produced by large objects colliding with our planet, and some of these objects may have been comets. (Others—perhaps the majority—may have been asteroids that wandered too far from the asteroid belt.) However, most of the craters are at least partially worn away by the action of wind and rain, which would indicate that many more craters, no longer visible, have existed on earth in the distant past, so that bombardment from space may occur even more often than the surviving craters indicate. The surface of the moon, which is not subject to erosion from wind and rain, is riddled with such craters, both large and small. Probably the surface of our planet would be riddled with craters as well if not for erosion.

Should we worry, then, that the earth may be hit by a large comet in the near future? No. Space is a big place, and the earth is actually rather tiny, astronomically speaking. Given the relatively low number of comets that we observe in the inner solar system each year, the odds against one of them actually colliding with our planet are comfortably small, if not exactly infinitesimal. Events such as the Tunguska explosion must be quite rare.

But what if the number of comets in the inner solar system were to increase? Would that also increase the chances of a collision between a comet and our planet? Yes, it would. Is there any evidence that the number of comets in the inner solar system was ever larger than it is today, or that it will increase in the future? Well, yes and no. There is no direct evidence that the number of comets changes, but if Raup and Sepkoski's theory of periodic extinctions is correct, then at times in the past the number of comets in the inner solar system must have increased nearly a thousandfold, and at such times the odds of a collision between the earth and a comet would have increased nearly to certainty.

Where do comets come from? This is a question that Halley could not answer; he could only tell us how existing comets behave, not how they got started on their peculiar orbital paths. But in 1950 the Dutch astronomer Jan Oort, borrowing in part from earlier theories by the Estonian astronomer Ernst Opik, suggested that our solar system was surrounded by a vast cloud of comets, which has subsequently come to be known as the *Oort cloud*.

Oort based this theory on the observation that many comets have orbits that take them as far as two lightyears from the sun—the distance that light travels in two years. Oort hypothesized that these comets, and probably others, had originated in a shell of material that orbited the sun at this distance, though many comets (such as Halley's) later had their orbits shortened by interaction with the gravity of large planets such as Jupiter.

This, in fact, is the shell of material we mentioned in the last chapter, left over from the original interstellar cloud that gave birth to our solar system and surrounding the solar system in a great ball. In the billions of years since the sun and planets formed, the material in this sphere has doubtlessly changed form somewhat, joining together into large chunks of ice and dust, perhaps one to 10 miles (1.6 to 16 km) in diameter, that occasionally fall inward toward the sun and become comets.

A few astronomers have suggested that this sphere of material may not be left over from the formation of the solar system but may have originally formed in the inner solar system, perhaps as part of the asteroid belt, where it was then gradually "perturbed" (deviating from its regular orbital motion) to the outer part of the solar system by the gravity of the large planets. Oort believed that the material was left over from a planet that exploded, though this theory is now largely discredited.

There is, in fact, no evidence that the Oort cloud exists at all; it remains only a scientific hypothesis, for which the support is persuasive but indirect. We can only guess what the cloud may be like: how big it is, how far from the sun, and so forth.

Some scientists have proposed that the cloud may contain material for 1 billion comets; a few have suggested that it may contain a hundred or even a thousand times as much. For the most part, this material remains in the outer solar system. Every now and then, however, something must happen to shake comets out of the cloud and send them plummeting toward the sun. (Some comets are probably shaken in the other direction, into interstellar space. It is possible that such comets may eventually be attracted by other stars and become part of their cometary systems. Some of the comets in orbit around our own sun may well have originated in other solar systems.)

What might disturb this cloud of comets? Although the Oort cloud is only about halfway from our sun to the nearest other star, Alpha Centauri, it is possible that in the distant past there have been stars that have wandered close enough to our sun to shake up the Oort cloud; possibly, they passed right through it. The gravitational attaction of such a star could have knocked millions of comets out of the Oort cloud and into the inner solar system. It is even possible that such "rogue stars" have been common visitors to the vicinity of our solar system in its 4½-billion-year existence, so that the inner solar system would have been continually resupplied with fresh comets.

It is not hard to imagine what havoc could be wreaked by a massive increase in the number of comets. As we pointed out earlier, an increase in the number of comets in the inner solar system would greatly increase the chance of a collision between the earth and a comet. Eventually, the large numbers of comets released by such a close encounter between the Oort cloud and a star would wear away as the comets dissolved in the heat of the sun—comets are mostly ice, remember—or as they collided with bodies in the inner solar system. But for a million years or so, the earth would find itself in a cosmic shooting gallery, and a comet that collided with the earth could have a devastating effect on living creatures here.

Comets, then, could conceivably be the cause of one or more of the mass extinctions in the earth's past. Is there evidence that any of the extinctions were caused by a collision with a comet or other object from space?

Yes, there is. And it turned up several years *before* Raup and Sepkoski noticed the periodic nature of such extinctions.

Chapter

4

The Iridium Anomaly

Walter Alvarez is a geologist, a scientist who studies the rocks of which our planet is made. In the late 1970s, he went to Italy to study samples of *sedimentary rock*, looking for clues to certain events in the earth's past. Ultimately, he found something he had not even been looking for.

What is sedimentary rock? It is rock formed by a process that takes place mostly at the bottoms of lakes, rivers and seas. Particles of material suspended in the water settle gradually to the bottom, where they form a deposit called sediment. Sediment may be composed of just about any material likely to be found in water, including animal skeletons, dust carried into the water by wind, weathered rocks worn away by erosion, and so forth. The combined pressure of water and additional layers of sediment eventually cements these particles together to form rock.

Sedimentary rock is valuable to paleontologists, geologists, and anyone else curious about conditions in the earth's distant past. Because it forms in layers, one on top of the other, it is possible to make a rough estimate of the age of a piece of sedimentary rock by its depth below the surface of the earth and by the types of fossils found in it. The layers of sedimentary rock, termed *strata* by those who study them, contain valuable clues to the condition of our planet at any point in time.

Alvarez, studying rock exposures in the mountains near the small town of Gubbio, Italy, examined strata of rocks laid down roughly at the end of the Cretaceous period, the time of the Great Cretaceous extinction—also known as "the Great Dying"—when the dinosaurs disappeared from the fossil record. Not surprisingly, he discovered a dramatic drop in the number of fossils embedded in the rock, right at the end of the Cretaceous period. However, he also noticed a change in the nature of the rock itself. Immediately above the Cretaceous rock was a layer of dull red clay about half an inch thick. Alvarez was not the first geologist to notice such a layer of clay in the rock strata, but his curiosity was sufficiently piqued by the clay that he took samples of it back to co-workers at the University of California.

There the clay was examined by his father, Nobel Prize-winning physicist Luis Alvarez. Chemical analysis showed that the clay was unusually rich in an element called iridium; in fact, it contained about thirty times as much iridium as might be found in normal rock strata.

Iridium is a fairly rare element—at least on the surface of the earth. It is far more common in the earth's molten core, 2,000 miles (3,200 km) below our feet. It is also fairly common in meteorites—chunks of rock from outer space.

Excited by this discovery, the Alvarezes teamed with two other scientists, Frank Asaro and Helen Michel, to

Luis Alvarez (left), professor of physics, emeritus, and Walter Alvarez, professor of geology, University of California in Berkeley, at the Cretaceous-Tertiary boundary

*A drawing of a dinosaur looking up at an asteroid in the sky.
Is it possible that this drawing depicts an actual scene at the
end of the Cretaceous period when the dinosaurs became extinct?*

try to find an explanation for this increased level of iridium in rock strata laid down immediately after the Cretaceous period. They ruled out the possibility that it came from the center of the earth because they were not aware of any mechanism that could bring the iridium to the surface (though some researchers have argued that volcanoes might be a possible mechanism). They also ruled out another hypothesis: that the iridium was scattered into the earth's atmosphere by a nearby exploding star. (The explosion of a star can produce a wide range of elements, iridium included.)

The only hypothesis they could not rule out was a collision between the earth and a large meteorite—a rocky body from space. On impact with the earth, such a meteorite could have splattered its iridium into the atmosphere, where it then would have gradually settled out to become part of the sedimentary strata. Where would such a meteorite have come from? The Alvarezes and their colleagues proposed that it was a large asteroid. Although most asteroids remain in the asteroid belt, between the orbits of Mars and Jupiter, astronomers have known for some time that a few asteroids actually wander inside the orbit of the earth and occasionally cross our planet's path. Because the first such asteroid discovered was named Apollo, all asteroids that cross the earth's orbit have become known as *Apollo asteroids*. The Alvarez team believed that this "iridium anomaly" was caused by a collision between the earth and an Apollo asteroid.

The fact that the anomaly occurred right at the end of the Cretaceous period, time of the most famous of all mass extinctions, could hardly have been coincidence. If the earth had collided with an asteroid at the end of the Cretaceous, then the asteroid may have contributed to the extinction.

The Alvarez team developed an elaborate explanation of how the asteroid collision might have resulted in the extinction. If the asteroid had struck on land, it would have raised a great cloud of dust; if it had struck in the ocean, it would have raised a cloud of steam. Either way, a cloud of material would have been projected into the earth's upper atmosphere, where it might have remained for months or even years.

This process has been observed in the eruption of volcanoes in the recent past, especially the eruption of the volcano Krakatoa in the nineteenth century. After Krakatoa erupted, particles of gas and dust remained in the earth's atmosphere for years, causing brilliant sunsets and darkening the days. By blocking the light from the sun, the debris from the Krakatoa explosion affected the weather on our planet. The year after the explosion of another volcano, Tambora (1815), came to be known as the "year without a summer." In the New England States, snow fell in June of that year.

The effect of the asteroid collision would have been similar but far worse. In fact, it would have been devastating to life on this planet. Sunlight would have been blocked almost entirely, and temperatures on earth would have plunged. A sudden change in climate resembling an ice age would have resulted. Many plants, which depend on sunlight for their energy, would have died. Small creatures that live near the surface of the ocean also would have been affected. As plants and small marine animals died, the animals that ate those plants and marine animals would have died, too, of starvation. And then the animals that ate the animals that ate the plants and marine animals would have died. And so forth. The *food chain* would have disintegrated.

The darkness itself might have had an effect on

some living creatures. Unable to see, the animals might have been unable to gather food or to go about their normal lives. (One piece of evidence for this hypothesis is that some dinosaurs living near the Arctic Circle—dinosaurs there would presumably have adapted to long periods of darkness—survived longer than dinosaurs from temperate zones.) Chaos would have ensued, with only the quickest, cleverest, and luckiest animals surviving the darkness. In fact, luck may have been the greatest selective factor in deciding which creatures survived this "asteroid winter" and which did not.

When the Alvarez team announced the theory in 1979, it met with a great deal of excitement in the scientific community. It also met with considerable controversy.

This was not the first time that someone had proposed an extraterrestrial explanation for the Cretaceous extinction; it was not even the first time an asteroid collision had been postulated as the cause. On the whole, however, paleontologists preferred to think of extinctions as arising from earthly causes. An asteroid—or anything from outer space, such as the explosion of a nearby star—was considered an unnecessary complication. Why bring in a disaster from outer space when the earth itself offered plenty of disasters with the potential for causing mass extinctions? In fact, why bring in a disaster at all, when slow processes of geological change were quite sufficient in themselves?

But the Alvarez team was the first to offer genuine physical evidence—the iridium anomaly—that the earth might have been profoundly affected by forces from space just at the end of the Cretaceous period. Still, there were many scientists who felt that the evidence was too flimsy: a single town in Italy where rock strata showed a high level of iridium.

Over the next few years, however, more evidence began to accumulate. Geologists examined rock strata in other parts of the world and found similar elevations in the level of iridium in strata from the end of the Cretaceous. The iridium anomaly was real, and pervasive, though that did not necessarily prove that the Alvarez team had properly interpreted its cause. Further, geologists have discovered glassy particles called *microtektites* that may have formed under extreme heat and pressure at about the time of the extinctions.

An objection made against the Alvarez theory was this: If there had been a major collision between the earth and an asteroid, it should have left a crater behind. The Cretaceous extinction was not a very long time ago, in geological terms: only about 65 million years. The crater, although it would have been considerably worn down by erosion, should still be visible. Yet of the dozens of known craters on the earth's surface, none appears to be from the end of the Cretaceous.

There are two possible answers to this objection. The first is that the asteroid might have fallen into the ocean, where any crater would have filled almost immediately with sediment. Therefore we can't find the crater because it never really existed, except perhaps for a brief moment after the collision.

Recently, another surprising piece of evidence for the Alvarez hypothesis has emerged. In samples of rock from roughly the same depth as the iridium layer discovered by the Alvarezes, scientists have now uncovered an unexpected concentration of carbon—the major element in the bodies of living organisms. The scientists theorize that this carbon, ten thousand times more abundant in these layers than in rock from other geological ages, is soot generated by massive fires at the end of the Cretaceous. Those fires, which may have been trig-

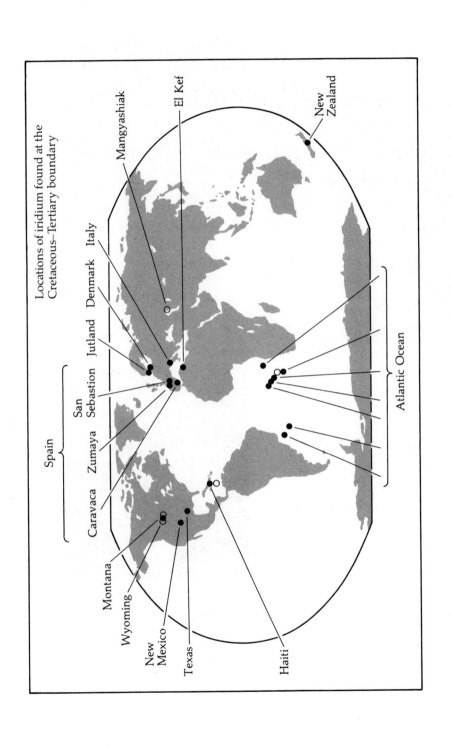

Locations of iridium found at the Cretaceous–Tertiary boundary

Mangyashiak

El Kef

New Zealand

Denmark Italy

Jutland

San Sebastion

Spain

Zumaya

Caravaca

Atlantic Ocean

Montana

Wyoming

New Mexico

Texas

Haiti

The demise of the dinosaurs is shown in this photograph, above, of exposed rock layers at Ash Creek, Montana. Scientists stand on the highest layer in which dinosaur fossils are found. To the right, a close-up of several centimeters of sediments marking the boundary between the Cretaceous and Tertiary periods at Stevens Klint, Denmark. The dark band is the boundary clay, containing unusually high levels of iridium and other rare elements.

gered by white-hot particles from the same extraterrestrial object believed responsible for the iridium layer, could have raged across entire continents, incinerating vast forests and filling the upper atmosphere with particles of soot. Although the soot would not have affected the earth's climate any more severely than the dust and steam thrown up by the Alvarezes' asteroid, it would have remained in the upper atmosphere for a longer period of time, producing a more devastating effect on the living organisms below.

The second answer is that the crater may have long ago disappeared below the surface of the earth, buried as a result of a process known as *subduction*. According to geologists, the crust of the earth—the outer "skin" of our planet—is made up of several more or less independent *plates*, each of which is floating on the semiliquid *mantle* underneath. Most of these plates are in motion, which accounts for the continuing rearrangement of the earth's continents that we call *continental drift*. Sometimes, at a place on the earth's surface known as a *subduction zone*, portions of one plate are swallowed up beneath another plate. The crater caused by the asteroid might have disappeared into a subduction zone in the 65 million years since the collision occurred.

The most important, and for the most part still unanswered, objection to the Alvarez theory is that it doesn't match the time frame in which the Cretaceous extinction is believed to have occurred. Paleontologists have long believed, based on the fossil evidence, that the dinosaurs and other species from the Cretaceous died out over a period of about a million years—a brief period of time to most paleontologists but not exactly overnight. Further, there were signs as early as the mid-Cretaceous—many millions of years before the extinction— that certain major species were becoming diminished, a fact that some paleontologists believe was an advance harbinger of the Cretaceous extinction itself.

If the Alvarez team is correct, however, the extinction must have been a very rapid event occurring over a period of a few years, perhaps even months. In paleontological terms, this is almost instantaneous and does not match the conventional interpretation of the fossil record.

Although no completely satisfactory answer has been made to this objection, there are several possible counterarguments. One is that the asteroid is merely one of several causes of the extinction—the straw (or perhaps boulder) that broke the dinosaur's back. Perhaps natural changes in the environment already had initiated a slow process of extinction that merely culminated with the arrival of the Alvarezes' asteroid. If the asteroid collision had not taken place, some species that otherwise would have become extinct might have outlived the Cretaceous. In fact, descendants of the dinosaurs might well be alive today.

It is also possible that the conventional interpretation of the fossil record is simply wrong. The dates assigned to mass extinctions are based in part on what paleontologists call *stratigraphic dating*, the dating of fossils according to the strata of rock in which they are found. We said earlier that it is possible to date sedimentary rocks according to their depth—or more precisely, their depth in relation to other strata of rock. Since rock strata are laid down one on top of the other by the sedimentation process, it is assumed that fossils found in lower strata are older than fossils found in higher strata. By cross-referencing the rock strata with other dating techniques, such as those based on the presence of radioactive elements in the skeletons of fossil animals, it is possible to assign dates to the various strata of rocks.

Thus, we can place a rough date on fossils based largely on the position of the strata of rock in which they appear, relative to other strata. But this dating technique is not altogether accurate; it allows us to date fossils within a tolerance of about 1 million years. Because stratigraphic dating is used extensively by paleontologists, it is difficult to determine precisely at what point in time the Cretaceous extinction took place or how long it took. Therefore, it is not impossible that an extinction that has heretofore been assumed to have taken place over a million-year period may in fact have taken place over a considerably shorter period if the accepted dates for the event are wrong. However, it is not enough for us to say blithely that the paleontologists have been mistaken all along in their assignment of dates; this sort of accusation must first be proved by careful research before it can be taken seriously.

Another argument in favor of the Alvarez theory is that the extinction might be the result of more than just a single collision with an asteroid or other body from space. Perhaps there were several such collisions over a period of time. While a single collision might not have been sufficient to cause the wholesale loss of species revealed by the fossil record, several collisions over the course of a million-year period might have been more than adequate, and this would explain why the Cretaceous extinction does not appear to be a sudden event. However, the Alvarez team may have hesitated to make such an assumption because the collision of an asteroid with the earth would seem to be a very rare event, and the possibility that more than one such collision took place over a million-year period would be highly unlikely.

But what if the iridium anomaly observed by the Alvarez team was the result not of a collision with an asteroid but a collision with a comet or comets? And what if it had occurred after some unusual event in the outer solar system had perturbed the Oort cloud, causing a rain of comets to descend on the inner solar system?

In that case, the idea of multiple collisions over a million-year period would seem much more likely, even inevitable. And what if the disturbance that knocked the comets out of the Oort cloud is a periodic event, occurring on a regular basis—say, once every 26 million years? Is it possible that not only the extinction of the dinosaurs but quite a few of the other mass extinctions indicated by the fossil record are caused when the earth is bombarded by comets?

It did not escape Raup and Sepkoski's attention that the Alvarez team's findings fit well with their own data. When they uncovered the evidence for periodic extinctions, among the first scientists they thought to share their data with were the Alvarezes.

Luis Alvarez has subsequently admitted that he was dubious when he first saw Raup and Sepkoski's data. But he shared the data with an associate, who analyzed it independently, and his analysis bore out Raup and Sepkoski's conclusion that the extinctions were indeed occurring on a periodic basis.

It occurred to Walter Alvarez, whose interest was engaged by these new findings, that if extinctions did occur periodically, and if these extinctions were the result of periodic bombardments by comets, then there also should be evidence that large craters on the earth's surface, caused by collisions with objects that might be comets (though they may also have been asteroids) should also occur on a periodic basis. With an associate, he analyzed a list of eighty-eight known craters to see if he could establish a pattern in their dates.

Unfortunately, not all of the craters on the list lent themselves to analysis. For some, the dates were not well known, and others fell outside the dates considered in Raup and Sepkoski's extinction graph. And Alvarez decided that the analysis should be restricted to craters at least 6 miles (9.6 km) in diameter; presumably objects that created smaller craters would not be likely to cause the global havoc necessary for a mass extinction.

This gave Alvarez a sample of thirteen craters to analyze—not a large sample but not too small to produce meaningful results. And the results appeared to be quite meaningful: after analysis, the craters seemed to have been formed at 28.4-million-year intervals, not that far from the 26-million-year extinction period uncovered by Raup and Sepkoski.

Excitedly, the Alvarezes called Raup and Sepkoski to give them the news. When Raup and Sepkoski performed their own analysis of the crater data, they got the same results as the Alvarezes.

Raup and Sepkoski were further helped along when geologists began to note iridium anomalies in strata connected with extinctions other than the one at the end of the Cretaceous, pointing to the conclusion that such extinctions were also caused by collisions with objects from outer space. The periodic-extinctions theory was looking better all the time.

Let us assume then that the extinctions and the craters are both periodic. That would seem to indicate that the periodic extinctions are caused by periodic bombardments of comets. Every 26 million years or so, this theory goes, the earth is pelted by dirty snowballs from space. Very *large* dirty snowballs from space. Dust and steam are projected into the upper atmosphere by the collisions. A miniature ice age descends on the earth after each collision. Thousands of species die.

This would nicely explain the observations of Raup and Sepkoski. But why should the Oort cloud be disturbed on a neat 26-million-year schedule? Where is the clock? What cosmic cycle would send showers of comets into the inner solar system on such a regular basis?

No one knows for sure, but the theories are fascinating indeed!

Chapter

5

Cosmic Debris, Death Stars, and Planet X

In many ways, the universe is like a giant clock. Intricate in design, its varied parts move together in a predictable harmony, a steady rhythm. Anyone sufficiently familiar with this rhythm can use the movement of objects in the sky to tell time, often with considerable accuracy. In fact, our very concept of time is based on the motion of objects in space—most notably, the motion of our own planet as it turns on its axis and orbits the sun.

The first time interval that primitive human beings must have been aware of is the day, the endlessly repeating cycle of day and night. Until a few centuries ago, it was believed that the day was the result of the rising and falling of the sun, which bestowed light upon a grateful humanity as it passed from horizon to horizon, then abandoned us to the darkness of night until it rose again the next morning.

In the middle of the sixteenth century, a Polish astronomer named Nicolaus Copernicus showed us that this was not the case. Actually, the earth was revolving on its own axis—an imaginary line extending through the planet from the North Pole to the South Pole—once every twenty-four hours, and the apparent motion of the sun through the skies was actually created by our own motion.

Because this cycle of night and day was extremely important, primitive people made the day the primary unit of timekeeping, though later this unit was broken down into hours, minutes, even seconds, when the necessity for more precise timekeeping arose. The hours, at least, could be measured, with the help of a device such as a sundial, by the motion of the sun through the sky. Sophisticated machines, such as clocks, with their own cyclical motion were needed to measure smaller intervals such as minutes and seconds.

Similarly, the cycle of the year and the seasons is caused by the earth's orbit around the sun. Astronomers can measure the passage of the seasons by observing the sun's movement through the distant stars in the sky. (Although these stars are not visible in the glare of sunlight during the day, they are indeed behind the sun.) In the course of the year, the sun passes through a range of constellations called the *zodiac*. Once again, however, this "motion" is only apparent and is the result of our planet's changing position relative to the sun as we revolve around it. Similarly, the changing seasons are caused by a tilt in the earth's position relative to the sun, which causes different parts of the planet to receive the bulk of the sun's light during different parts of the year.

These cycles are very regular and very predictable because they are the product of fixed natural laws and forces. The revolution of the earth around the sun, for instance, is the product of two forces: the earth's *inertia* (its tendency to move through space in a straight line at a fixed speed) and the sun's gravity (which bends the earth's straight-line motion into a circular orbit). These forces are of constant, unchanging strength. Because the earth's motion in space is the result of these unchanging forces, it never changes either. (This is not to say that the application of some unexpected outside force could not alter the earth's motion around the sun, but to the best of our knowledge this has never happened—and we can hope that it never does because the results would be disastrous!)

There are many such cyclical motions in the universe, all of them produced by the interactions of forces as prescribed by the laws of physics. Rotation, in particular, seems to be a common feature of the universe. Each of the other planets in the solar system rotates on its axis, just as the earth does. Our galaxy also rotates, which probably explains its spiral structure. As the galaxy rotates, our solar system moves on its own path through the body of the galaxy.

Often, this rotating motion takes our sun through the galactic plane. (See Chapter Two.) Because the galactic plane represents the vertical center of our galaxy, it is the point where the collective gravity of all of the matter in the galaxy is strongest. That is why cosmic debris tends to settle out in the galactic plane, in much the same way as bilge water settles out in the lowest portion of a boat (because that puts it closest to the earth's center of gravity).

Our solar system is also attracted toward the galactic plane, but it doesn't settle out there. Instead, it bobs up and down, like a buoy in stormy waters, passing through the galactic plane once on the upstroke and again on the downstroke. Because one complete "bob" takes 62 million years, the solar system passes through the galactic plane once every 31 million years.

Some astronomers, when they first heard of Raup and Sepkoski's 26-million-year extinction period, immediately thought of the solar system's motion relative to the galactic plane. Although 31 million years and 26 million years may seem rather far apart, the two periods were sufficiently similar to imply the possibility of some kind of relationship. Furthermore, some others who have studied Raup and Sepkoski's data believe that the extinction period is longer than they have suggested, perhaps as long as 31 million years.

Two such astronomers are Michael R. Rampino and Richard B. Stothers, who published a paper in the April 19, 1984, issue of the British science journal *Nature*, indicating that they had not only found a 29- to 31-million-year cycle in extinctions, based on the same data used by Raup and Sepkoski, but had found what they felt was a 31-million-year period in large craters, which suggests that the craters and the extinctions might both be connected with the solar system's periodic visits to the galactic plane.

According to their calculations, if our solar system were to pass near a large gas cloud of the sort thought to be common in the galactic plane, the gravitational attraction of the cloud would be sufficient to disturb the Oort cloud and jar loose a shower of comets. They also suggest that if the solar system were to pass through the cloud itself, it could pollute the earth's atmosphere with hydrogen, which could have an effect on climate. Furthermore, since the sun "burns" hydrogen as its fusion fuel, the passage of the solar system through a hydrogen cloud might increase the heat of the sun, which would further affect the climate on Earth. Such climate effects could either contribute to mass extinctions already triggered by a comet shower or produce mass extinctions of their own.

In the same issue of *Nature* (which contains several articles in response to Raup and Sepkoski's findings), physicists Richard D. Schwartz and Philip B. James of the University of Missouri offer a powerful objection to the galactic plane theory: the timing is wrong. Although the mass extinctions have occurred on a cycle similar to that of the solar system's oscillations—that is, up and down motions—in the galaxy, they occurred at the wrong part of the oscillation, when the sun is at its farthest point from the galactic plane. However, they also point out that the amount of radiation the earth receives from outer space might vary according to our position within the galaxy, with the radiation falling off as our solar system approaches its maximum distance from the galactic plane. Perhaps, they imply, the loss of radiation might have negative effects on the environment, so that extinctions would occur when the sun was *farthest* from the galactic plane.

Perhaps the most exciting theory proposed in answer to Raup and Sepkoski's data is the so-called death star theory, which suggests that our sun may have a hitherto unseen companion that passes through the Oort cloud once every 26 million years.

Most stars that we can see in the sky, either with our naked eyes or through telescopes, are part of *multiple-star systems*. As the name implies, a multiple-star system is a solar system in which there is more than one sun. Bound together by their mutual gravitational attraction, these suns orbit one another much as planets orbit stars.

Our sun is not part of such a system—or so most astronomers have believed. However, several teams of researchers have proposed just such a system as the cause of the hypothetical comet bombardments from the Oort cloud.

The first such team was composed of Daniel P. Whitmire, an astrophysicist at the University of Southwestern Louisiana, and Albert A. Jackson, IV of Computer Sciences Corporation in Houston, Texas. The members of the second team were Marc Davis and Richard A. Muller of the University of California, Berkeley, and Piet Hut of the Institute for Advanced Study in Princeton, New Jersey.

Both teams put forth a similar theory. What if the sun has a small companion star that orbits it at a considerable distance, periodically—once every 26 million years—drawing close enough to the Oort cloud to shake loose some comets?

Why have we never seen this star? Because it is dark and far away. Most likely, it is either a *brown dwarf* or a *white dwarf.*

A brown (or black) dwarf is a star that was not large enough to generate sufficient internal heat for fusion reactions to start; essentially, it is a protostar that never quite became a real star. Having exhausted all of its original friction heat, it is now a dark lump of cooling material. Nonetheless, it may be large enough to perturb the Oort cloud. (Some astronomers have suggested that the planet Jupiter is a brown dwarf star, or nearly so. If Jupiter had been only a little larger than it is, it might have been able to generate sufficient internal heat to become a protostar and perhaps even a real star.)

A white dwarf star is a star that has lived a full life as a normal star but has run out of fusion fuel and collapsed under its own considerable weight. Still hot and glowing, such a white dwarf also would be extremely dense because it would contain all of the material of a full-fledged star packed into a body about the size of the earth. It would produce a considerable amount of gravity and would be quite capable of shaking up the Oort cloud.

Where would this star be? Perhaps more than thirty thousand times as far from the sun as the earth is—a considerable distance. Its orbit would be elliptical, stretched out, like the orbit of a comet.

When would such a companion star have come into existence? There is considerable argument about that. Perhaps it was born at the same time as the rest of the solar system, out of the cloud from which the sun and planets formed; it might have been born in much the same manner as a planet.

However, Piet Hut has recently reconsidered the orbit of such a companion star. His latest analysis shows that the orbit of the star would be highly unstable because it would travel so far from our sun it could easily be trapped by the gravitation of another star and vanish from our solar system entirely. Other scientists who have calculated possible orbits for the companion star suggest that it might be able to remain stable for as long as a billion years but not for the full lifetime of our solar system, which is generally assumed to be 4.6 billion years.

A possible response to this objection is that the companion star was not originally part of our solar system. Perhaps it was a wandering star that was "captured" by our sun a few hundred million years ago. Or perhaps it *was* always part of the solar system but was originally in a more stable orbit. Then, sometime in the last billion years, something happened to jar it into its current configuration. Either way, the companion star would seem to be a peculiar star indeed, and our solar system would not resemble any other star system observed to date by astronomers.

SEARCH FOR 'NEMESIS' INTENSIFIES DEBATE OVER EXTINCTIONS

The Sun's small companion star, if it exists, should now be at outermost point in its orbit and some three light years away, according to theory.

NEMESIS
(PRESENT
POSITION)

How a Star Can Cause Devastation
New fossil studies suggest that mass extinctions not only wiped out the dinosaurs long ago but occur regularly on Earth every 26 million years. The Nemesis hypothesis is one of the more imaginative explanations of how celestial forces could be the cause.

From the front page of The New York Times's *science section,* Science Times, *an article explaining the death star theory*

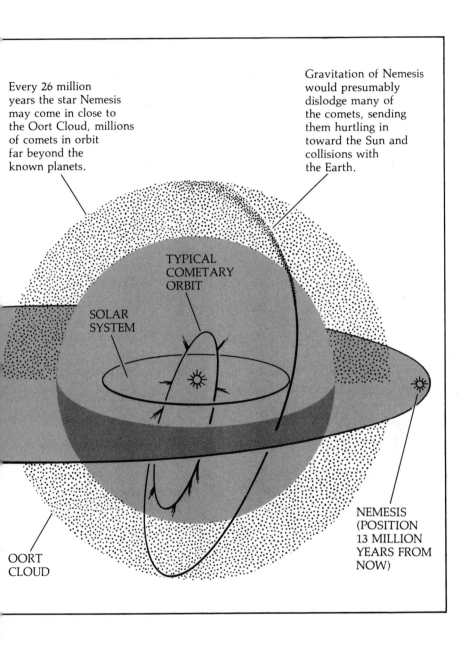

Every 26 million years the star Nemesis may come in close to the Oort Cloud, millions of comets in orbit far beyond the known planets.

Gravitation of Nemesis would presumably dislodge many of the comets, sending them hurtling in toward the Sun and collisions with the Earth.

TYPICAL COMETARY ORBIT

SOLAR SYSTEM

OORT CLOUD

NEMESIS (POSITION 13 MILLION YEARS FROM NOW)

If the companion star exists, then we should be able to see it through a telescope. How will we go about finding it?

As it happens, the hypothetical companion star may already have been photographed by a telescope on board a satellite. The InfraRed Astronomical Satellite (or I.R.A.S. for short) was launched in 1983 to take pictures of the heavens using infrared light. Although it was in orbit for only ten months, the I.R.A.S. took pictures of 250,000 objects, and those pictures are waiting for scientists to comb through them, looking for the companion star. In fact, this combing has already begun.

And how will scientists know the companion star when they see it? The answer is *parallax*, the change in position of an object relative to its background when viewed from two different angles. If you hold your hand in front of your face and look at it first with just your left eye and then with just your right eye, it will seem to shift position against a distant wall or landscape. This shift is called parallax; it is the way our brains distinguish between nearby objects and distant objects, giving us three-dimensional vision. In the same way, a nearby star will shift position relative to more distant stars when viewed from different points in the earth's orbit around the sun because we will be viewing it from different angles. Most stars are too far away for any parallax to be noted, but the companion star would be closer to earth than any other star except our sun and therefore would demonstrate the most dramatic parallax. The trick then is to look at two pictures taken of the same portion of the sky at different times of the year and look for stars that have moved between photographs. Any star that moves is a strong candidate for the companion star.

Finally, if the companion star *is* found, what will we call it?

The Davis, Hut, and Muller team suggests the name Nemesis, "after the Greek goddess who relentlessly persecutes the excessively rich, proud and powerful"—presumably a reference to the dinosaurs, who were the dominant species on this planet before they were cut down by the Cretaceous extinction.

Paleontologist Stephen Jay Gould, however, argues for the name Siva, after the Hindu god of destruction. Why? Because, according to Gould, Siva doesn't attack or destroy particular targets. Instead, Siva is responsible for maintaining order in our world. In short, if the companion star exists and if it indeed causes periodic rains of comets and mass extinctions, then it has played a significant role in making our world what it is today, and it is part of the natural process we call evolution.

Yet another theory, similar to the death star theory, is that our solar system has a tenth planet, beyond Pluto, that can act to perturb the Oort cloud.

The idea that there is another, as yet undiscovered planet in our solar system is not new. Certain oddities in the orbit of Neptune have long suggested that it might be disturbed in some way by the gravitational pull of some unseen object at the edge of the solar system. When the planet Pluto was discovered in 1930, it was thought to be the source of those disturbances. However, Pluto is now regarded by some astronomers as too small to have such an effect on Neptune. (A few astronomers have suggested that the Oort cloud may be responsible for disturbing the orbit of Neptune.) Could there be another planet in the solar system?

Daniel P. Whitmire and John Matese, at the University of Southwestern Louisiana, suggest that Planet X, as they call it, may be so far out on the fringes of the solar system that it periodically crosses through the Oort cloud and knocks comets out of their orbits. Planet X would be about one hundred times as far from the sun as the earth is, and its orbit would be tilted at something of an angle relative to the rest of the solar system.

Why would the Planet X theory be superior to the companion star theory in explaining the periodic extinctions? Well, for one thing, it isn't a new idea; it has a long astronomical tradition, and the evidence for it has already been noted. On the other hand, there is no previous basis for believing in the existence of Nemesis/Siva.

Second, its orbit would be more stable than that of Nemesis because it would be closer to the sun and less likely to be snagged by the gravitational pull of a passing star.

Chapter

6

The Consensus

There is little question that the theory of periodic extinctions has created considerable excitement in the scientific community. In a way, it would almost be a pity if it turned out not to be true. It is an elegant theory—it explains a great deal with moderate effort. In one fell swoop it provides an explanation for ten mass extinctions, and possibly more if the theory can be extended to earlier extinctions than the one at the end of the Permian period.

But elegance and excitement are not substitutes for truth, and they must not blind us to the fact that this theory has yet to win acceptance in that same scientific community. Raup and Sepkoski, like the Alvarezes before them, have given us a tantalizing clue to events in the mysterious past, a clue with striking and far-reaching ramifications but still only a clue for all of that. Is there a death star? Does the Oort cloud periodically shower the inner solar system with deadly comets? Did

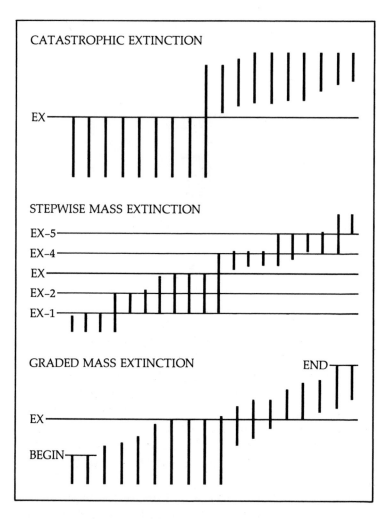

These graphs illustrate the three theories of mass extinctions now being debated. A catastrophic extinction results from some event that destroys many different species within a very short time. A graded mass extinction, the classic theory of paleontologists and biologists, happens gradually over a few million years. A stepwise mass extinction has a number of short-term extinctions occurring over a period of 3 million years. Some, but not all, of these are caused by catastrophic events.

the dinosaurs pass away in the cold and the dark of some terrible cosmic night?

In truth, we may never know. The past occasionally relinquishes its secrets, but it hides far more than it reveals. The fossil record contains the story of life on earth, but it is often couched in cryptic language, and we can only guess at its meaning. Does the sudden jump in iridium after the Cretaceous tell us that the earth collided with an asteroid or a comet? Maybe it does; the Alvarezes believe so. But maybe it tells us something else altogether.

Charles B. Officer and Charles L. Drake of Dartmouth College argue, in the March 8, 1985, issue of *Science* magazine that the iridium layer is of purely earthly origin and that no comets need be invoked to explain it. Where did this iridium come from? From volcanoes, which released the iridium contained deep within the earth.

According to Officer and Drake, the mixture of foreign elements in the post-Cretaceous clay is much closer to that found in the earth's mantle—the half-liquid, half-solid layer of material that lies beneath the earth's crust—than it is to the elements found in meteorites and other bodies from space. They also point out that the layer of clay that contains the iridium is quite thick and must have been laid down over a period tens of thousands of years in length. If the iridium had been released to the atmosphere by the impact of a single asteroid, it should have settled out in a few decades, at most a few centuries. The long interval over which the iridium level was increased speaks more of a period of increased volcanic activity than of a single asteroid (or comet) collision.

And what of the microtektites—the glassy shards apparently formed by the heat and pressure of the asteroid's impact? Officer and Drake attribute them to forces within the earth rather than on the earth's surface. By way of example, they point to similar materials formed by natural geological processes. Such materials also could have been ejected by a volcanic eruption and thus would naturally accompany the increase in iridium.

Is there other evidence of such a period of volcanic activity occurring at roughly the end of the Cretaceous? Yes, say Officer and Drake. An immense lava field in India is filled with materials apparently expelled from the earth over a short period, roughly 60 to 65 million years ago by the best available estimate. Similarly, another lava field in Siberia contains evidence that a similar period of volcanism occurred at the end of the Permian period, which could prove that volcanic activity is tied to more than one mass extinction.

Proponents of the impact theory of extinction have not let such objections go unanswered, of course. As for the thickness of the iridium layer, for instance, some scientists argue that the iridium could have been spread through a wider area than it originally occupied by the action of plants and their roots burrowing through the soil or by some natural but incompletely understood sedimentation process. And, argues Bruce Bohor of the U.S. Geological Survey, the microtektite crystals dating from the Cretaceous extinction are quite unlike those known to be produced on earth.

Antoni Hoffman of Columbia University, writing in the June 20, 1985, issue of *Nature*, argues that the method by which Raup and Sepkoski assigned dates to the mass extinctions they found in the fossil record was too arbitrarily chosen and that perfectly valid alternative methods of assigning the dates would produce results showing no periodic extinctions at all.

Further, Hoffman attacks the very statistical foundation on which Raup and Sepkoski have based their theory. According to Hoffman, the method used by Raup and Sepkoski to define what constitutes a "mass extinction" is itself biased toward periodicity—that is, the existence of periodic cycles—and the cyclical quality they discovered lies as much in the statistical mathematics with which they analyzed their data as in the data itself.

This argument deserves closer scrutiny because it has become the basis for several additional articles refuting the periodic extinctions theory. The argument goes like this: When Raup and Sepkoski drew their graph of extinction events over the last 250 million years, they divided that time period into intervals of 6.2 million years apiece. They defined a mass extinction as any such interval in which the number of extinctions was higher than in both the preceding and following intervals. In other words, if one 6.2-million-year interval contains 120 extinctions, it qualifies as a mass extinction only if the intervals immediately before and after it both contain fewer than 120 extinctions. The actual number of extinctions in an interval is irrelevant; what is important is how the number of extinctions in that interval relates to the number in the surrounding intervals.

Hoffman argues that any interval on the graph has precisely a twenty-five percent chance of being a mass extinction interval using Raup and Sepkoski's criteria. How so? As Hoffman points out, there is a fifty percent chance that any interval will be preceded by an interval with fewer extinctions and a fifty percent chance that it will be followed by an interval with fewer extinctions. Thus, every interval has a twenty-five percent chance of being both preceded and followed by an interval of fewer extinctions and thereby being declared a mass extinction interval—even if Raup and Sepkoski were using random data.

It follows, then, that mass extinctions will be found, on average, in every fourth interval. Four times the length of a single interval on the graph is 24.8 million years, strikingly close to the 26-million-year period noted by Raup and Sepkoski. Thus, Hoffman declares that the so-called periodic extinctions are merely a figment of the mathematics used to verify their existence.

But Stephen Jay Gould, writing in the November 1985 issue of *Discover* magazine, points out that Raup and Sepkoski did not claim to have found mass extinction events on an average of every 26 million years. They claimed to have found extinction events *every* 26 million years, which is quite a different thing. Gould compares this to the statistical probability of flipping a coin and having it come up either heads or tails. If you flip a coin often enough, the laws of probability say that it will come up tails every other flip, on average. But it won't come up tails neatly on alternate flips: heads, tails, heads, tails, heads, tails, etc. If it does, then something is very wrong. Hence, Raup and Sepkoski have found, according to Gould, a genuine paleontological anomaly, one that is not inherent in the mathematics of their calculations.

One of the most persistent critics of both Raup and Sepkoski and the Alvarezes has been Anthony Hallam of the University of Birmingham in England. Like many paleontologists, Hallam objects that the fossil record is not consistent with the notion that extinctions such as that at the end of the Cretaceous were sudden, dramatic events precipitated by a catastrophic asteroid collision. Although a great many species disappeared at the end of the Cretaceous, quite a few—such as birds, mammals, and reptiles—survived in substantial numbers. Why should those species have come through the disaster nearly unscathed when others were eliminated from the fossil record altogether?

Hallam also suggests that the change in the mineral composition of the clay right at the end of the Cretaceous may be the *result* of the extinctions, not a symptom of their cause. The sediment in the rocks just below this clay is made in large part from the fossilized bones of ancient fish. Because many of those fish might have died in the extinction, it is only natural that the nature of the rock would change at precisely that point.

To fill any void left in the absence of the asteroid/comet theory, Hallam offers an alternative explanation for the great mass extinctions indicated by the fossil record: changes in sea level. Hallam has compiled a graph (see page 78) that shows how most major extinction events occurred at times when the geological record shows evidence of a major and sudden drop in the level of the oceans. Ocean-dwelling species might have been killed by sudden reduction of their habitats; land-dwellers, in turn, might have been affected by related changes in climate.

To the uninitiated, it might seem strange that so many scientists can find so many different ways to interpret what would seem to be the same body of evidence. Why is there so much disagreement? Why can't they look at the facts—at the fossil evidence pried with great effort from the rocks of the earth—and divine from them the truth of what happened millions and millions of years ago? If the evidence is for periodic extinctions, then why can't they simply accept the evidence and declare that the periodic extinctions happened?

Alas, things are not so simple. Science is rarely a

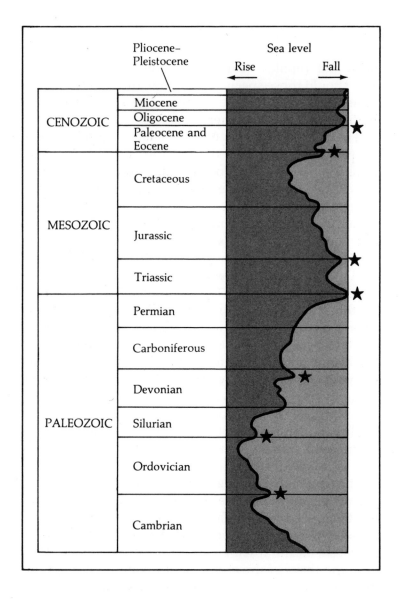

Global sea level over the past 570 million years.
Notice the coincidence between mass extinctions (asterisks)
and times of marked change in sea level.

matter of neatly arrayed evidence and obvious facts. More often, it is a matter of confusing, contradictory evidence and a painfully won consensus among scientists as to which pieces of evidence should be taken seriously and which should be ignored as irrelevant. But the road to such a consensus can be a rocky one, and there is no general agreement on how it should be reached.

Robert Jastrow, writing in the September 1983 issue of *Science Digest*, tells of the reaction of physicist Luis Alvarez, father of the impact extinction theory, when confronted by the objections of paleontologists who felt that the iridium anomaly was not sufficient to explain the Cretaceous extinction. "I simply do not understand why some paleontologists . . . deny that there was ever a catastrophic extinction," Alvarez reportedly declared. "I'm really quite puzzled [that] knowledgeable paleontologists would show such a lack of appreciation for the scientific method."

According to Jastrow, "Professor Alvarez was pulling rank on the paleontologists. Physicists sometimes do that; they feel they have a monopoly on clear thinking. There is a power in their use of math and the precision of their measurements that transcends the power of the softer sciences."

Jastrow goes on to say that scientists often rank the various branches of science according to the precision with which they can achieve experimental results. Physics and mathematics—the so-called hard sciences—are extremely precise; they produce results that are often about as unambiguous as any science could be expected to produce. They are perennially at the top of such a scientific ranking. The "soft" sciences, such as psychology and anthropology, on the other hand, rarely produce unambiguous results, and so they are somehow held in lower esteem, especially by physicists and mathematicians.

Paleontology falls somewhere in between. It is not that the paleontologists lack hard evidence of the ways in which living creatures evolved on this planet in ages past; it is that they have too much. Paleontologists must wade through mounds of ambiguous, often contradictory clues as to how life developed, and the interpretation of those clues is often as much a matter of personal judgment and inspired guesswork as it is a question of applying hard mathematical analysis to the evidence.

What makes the periodic extinctions theory so interesting is that it represents a wedding of paleontology and two traditionally "harder" sciences—physics and astronomy. And though a physicist such as Alvarez may feel that the hard evidence of the iridium atoms detected in the clay laid down after the Cretaceous extinctions is sufficient to prove that those extinctions were the result of a catastrophic event, the paleontologists feel differently. They know that the past does not yield its secrets so easily or so unambiguously. Even so seemingly precise a clue as the iridium anomaly is open to dozens of different interpretations, and every single one of them might be wrong—or right.

Yet, ironically, it may turn out to be just such a precise clue that wins the day for the theories of Raup and Sepkoski and the Alvarezes. If Nemesis/Siva, the predicted companion star, does indeed exist, in more or less the orbit that the extinction data would place it in, it will be powerful evidence in favor of the periodic extinctions theory and will go a long way toward convincing even the feisty and independent paleontologists that their previous interpretations of the fossil record were wrong. Even so, it is doubtful that anything approaching a scientific consensus will be achieved overnight.

The big-brained dinosaur of the late Cretaceous, Stenonycho-saurus inequalus. Its ratio of brain weight to body weight equaled that of early mammals. Had such dinosaurs lived on, they might have halted the rise of mammals.

More likely, the final consensus will be won only after years of arguing and analyzing evidence. In time, the theories of Raup and Sepkoski may be forgotten, consigned to the limbo of scientific theories that were elegant and exciting but unsupported by the facts. Or they may win increasing support until they are the accepted picture of what actually went on in the prehistoric past. They may never be proved, in the sense that Newton's laws of motion can be said to be "proved," and even if they are accepted, they may eventually be superseded by a better, or at least more accurate, view of the past.

It is important, though, that we do not rush to judgment on such things. If we find that life on earth is indeed at the mercy of impersonal astronomical events, then it will alter the very way we perceive the nature of life. Until recently, most scientists believed that life evolved on this planet as part of a complex and grandiose process of constant and gradual change. Instead, this process may be horrifyingly random. Evolution may hinge on a cosmic dice game in which luck is the chief criterion for survival. The grandiose process, the grand design of life, may be nothing more than a chaotic series of extinctions in which the ecological niches are emptied by impersonal catastrophes and filled by opportunistic organisms taking advantage of the fate of their luckless brethren. Of course, if it weren't for those impersonal disasters, intelligent life might never have had a chance to develop on our planet, and so perhaps we should be grateful that they happened, if indeed they happened at all. However, this also implies that intelligent life might be rare in the universe, the product of an improbable series of events that may have been duplicated nowhere else in the cosmos. Perhaps, then, we are alone in the universe.

Or perhaps this is too harsh a view. Regardless, science is obliged to take its time about adopting such a vision of our planet's history, to assess all of the evidence before coming forth with its judgment.

The consensus will come in time, of course. It always does.

Epilogue

When the Alvarezes first published their theory that the Cretaceous extinction was the result of a collision between the earth and an asteroid, it caught the imagination of a group of scientists interested more in the future of our planet than in its past.

Would it be possible, they asked themselves, for such disastrous changes in the earth's climate to be brought about not by the impact of an asteroid or a comet but by some more terrestrial catastrophe—such as the explosion of a few hydrogen bombs?

Yes, they answered. It would be possible. In fact, according to their calculations, it wouldn't even take terribly many bombs. A small nuclear war—an exchange of missiles between, say, the United States and the Soviet Union—might eject sufficient dust into the upper atmosphere to blot out the sun and plunge the earth into a nuclear winter far more devastating than the asteroid or comet winter that killed the dinosaurs. In fact, the nuclear winter might leave no life at all on the planet, except for bacteria adapted to survival in icy climates, plants with seeds that can survive in frozen soil, and perhaps a few species of insect.

To future paleontologists—given time, even insects can evolve into paleontologists—it would be a gap in the fossil record even more dramatic than the one at the end of the Permian. Perhaps then they would wonder at, and debate, and eventually reach a consensus on the reasons why this particular extinction arrived 13 million years ahead of schedule.

Glossary

Apollo asteroids—Asteroids with irregular orbits that sometimes cross the orbit of our planet.

Asteroid belt—The area between the orbits of Mars and Jupiter in which can be found a large number of orbiting chunks of rocks called asteroids.

Big bang—The explosion, believed by astronomers to have occurred about 15 billion years ago, that gave birth to our universe.

Brown drawf—A star-like body that never produced enough energy to trigger fusion processes and therefore never became a full-fledged star.

Catastrophism— The idea that changes in living organisms over the history of the earth are the result of sudden catastrophes, or "revolutions"; generally attributed to the 19th century anatomist Georges Cuvier.

Comet—A body made out of ice and dust, orbiting the sun in a highly irregular orbit that takes it occasionally so close to the sun that it may produce a bright "tail" under the influence of the energetic particles streaming outward from the sun.

Continental drift—The process by which the plates that make up the earth's surface drift on the mantle underneath, leading to (among other things) the rearrangement of the two continents that existed on earth tens of millions of years ago into the several continents that we know today.

Craters—A hole on the ground formed by the impact of a meteorite.

Ecological niche—The manner in which a species of living organism makes its "living" within its environment, i.e. the kinds of food it eats, the way in which it gathers that food, the way it gives birth to and nurtures its young, and so forth.

Evolution—The process of gradual change by which species of living organisms give rise to new species of living organisms over a period of many generations.

Extinction—The death of an entire species of living organism.

Food chain—The sequence by which the energy produced by the sun finds its way into the earth's food supplies, beginning with plants which "trap" that energy through photosynthesis, continuing through the animals that eat the plants, and on through the animals that eat those animals, and so forth.

Fossil record—The buried remains of once-living organisms, in which scientists can read the history of life on this planet.

Fusion—The process by which several atoms, commonly hydrogen atoms, are fused together to form a smaller number of larger atoms, such as helium. Energy is given off by this process, which is the source of energy behind all but the youngest stars.

Galactic plane—The imaginary plane extending through the middle of a galaxy, with its outer edges bisecting the outermost fringes of the galaxy on all sides and its middle passing through the galactic center.

Galaxy—A very large swarm of stars held together by gravity, usually in the shape of an immense spiral or disk.

Gradualism—The idea that changes in species of living organisms over the history of the earth were the result of gradual processes of change.

Hydrogen—The most abundant chemical element in the universe.

Iridium—A rare element found in rock strata and an element common in meteorites.

Iridium anomaly—More than normal amounts of iridium found in the earth's rock.

Light-year—The distance lights travels in a year, commonly used as a measure of interstellar distances, roughly equal to 9,460 billion kilometers.

Mantle—The semi-liquid material beneath the earth's surface on which the surface plates float.

Mass extinction—A period in the history of the earth, extending over at most three or four million years, during which an unusually large number of extinctions occurs.

Microtektites—Glassy particles in rock strata that form under extreme heat and pressure.

Multiple star system—A solar system containing more than one sun.

Nuclear winter—The period of cold and darkness that many scientists now believe would result from a nuclear war and the resulting environmental devastation.

Oort cloud—The sphere of frozen gases and other materials surrounding the solar system at a distance of about one to two light-years, believed to be the source of comets.

Orbit—A circular path taken by an object in space bound gravitationally by another object, but with sufficient sideways momentum not to collide with that object.

Paleontologists—Scientists who study the history of living organisms in the distant past of the planet Earth.

Parallax—The change in position of an object relative to its background when viewed from two different angles.

Periodic mass extinctions—The theory that mass extinctions occur on a regular basis, roughly once every 26 million years, for reasons that have not yet been determined.

Planet X—The term for a possible tenth planet in our solar system.

Plates—The free-floating divisions of the earth's surface.

Protostar—A young star in which heat is produced by gravitational energy rather than fusion.

Satellite—A man-made vehicle that can orbit around space.

Sedimentary rock—Rock produced by a process called sedimentation, in which tiny particles deposited in water settle to the bottom and are slowly cemented together into solid rock.

Solar system—Our sun and all objects in orbit around it, including planets, asteroids, and comets.

Spectroscope—An instrument for breaking a ray of light into its component wavelengths, or colors, usually to determine chemical composition of materials through which the light has passed.

Strata—Layers of sedimentary rock.

Stratigraphic dating—The process by which paleontologists determine the age of a fossil by the geological stratum—that is, layer of sedimentary rock—in which it was found.

Subatomic particles—Particles that are smaller than atoms.

Subduction—A geological process by which the floating plates that make up the earth's surface slide underneath one another to produce material which may later become part of new plates.

T tauri wind—The stream of subatomic particles produced by our sun at the end of its protostar stage, which blew away the atmospheres of the four inner planets of the solar system.

White dwarf—A star that has burned all of its fusion fuel and no longer produces energy, though it may still have sufficient heat left over from earlier stages of its existence to produce light.

Further Reading

Allaby, Michael, and Lovelock, James. *The Great Extinction*. New York: Doubleday, 1983.

Cloud, Preston. *Cosmos, Earth and Man*. New Haven, Connecticut: Yale University Press, 1978.

Colbert, Edwin H. *The Age of Reptiles*. New York: W.W. Norton, 1965.

Halstead, L.B. *The Search for the Past*. New York: Doubleday, 1982.

Index

Sea level theory of extinc-
tion, 77, *78*
Sedimentary rock, 43–44
Sepkoski, John, Jr., 15–16,
17, *18*, 19–20, 38
criticism and support
of theories, 56, 57,
58, 74–77
Siva, 69, 80
Solar system, 27–30, 61–
63, 69
Spectroscopes, 22
Stars, 40, 60, 63
types of, 64–65
Stratigraphic dating, 54–
55
Strothers, Richard B., 62
Subatomic particles, 29
Subduction, 53

Sun, 23, 25, 61, 63
creation of, 25–27, 28

Telescopes, 21–22, 68
T tauri wind, 29

Universe
creation of, 21
cycles in, 59–62
study of, 21–22

Volcanoes, 29, 47, 48,
73–74

Whipple, Fred, 31
Whitmire, Daniel P., 64,
70

Zodiac, 60